Munroe Smith

Bismarck and German Unity

Vol. 1

Munroe Smith

Bismarck and German Unity
Vol. 1

ISBN/EAN: 9783337377793

Printed in Europe, USA, Canada, Australia, Japan

Cover: Foto ©ninafisch / pixelio.de

More available books at **www.hansebooks.com**

BISMARCK

AND

GERMAN UNITY

A HISTORICAL OUTLINE

BY

MUNROE SMITH

DOCTOR OF LAWS OF GÖTTINGEN UNIVERSITY
PROFESSOR OF ROMAN LAW AND COMPARATIVE JURISPRUDENCE
IN COLUMBIA UNIVERSITY

New York

PUBLISHED FOR THE COLUMBIA UNIVERSITY PRESS BY

THE MACMILLAN COMPANY

LONDON: MACMILLAN & CO., LTD.

1898

Norwood Press
J. S. Cushing & Co. — Berwick & Smith
Norwood Mass. U.S.A.

PREFACE

THIS sketch of Prince Bismarck's work was published, immediately after his death, in the New York *Evening Post* and (in part) in *The Nation*. It is reprinted with little change and with few additions. It would have been easy to expand the sketch into a portly volume, — easier, indeed, than it was originally to keep it within its present limits, — but it is believed that such a summary as is here offered will be useful to those who are too busy to read many thick books, and to those who wish a more sharply outlined impression than is readily obtained from a mass of details. It will be most useful, however, if it awakens in some readers the interest in a great career which the writer has felt for a quarter of a century, and if it sets them to reading other and fuller histories.

MUNROE SMITH

COLUMBIA UNIVERSITY, September 6, 1898

CONTENTS

From the beginning of my career I have had but the one guiding star: By what means and in what way can I bring Germany to unity? and in so far as this end has been attained: How can I strengthen this unity and increase it and give it such form that it shall be enduringly maintained with the free consent of all coöperating forces? — BISMARCK IN THE GERMAN IMPERIAL DIET, JULY 9, 1879

BISMARCK

AND

GERMAN UNITY

OTTO EDWARD LEOPOLD VON BISMARCK was born at Schönhausen in the Old Mark of Brandenburg, province of Saxony, kingdom of Prussia, April 1, 1815. He came of a line of country gentle- men, whose main business was always the care of their estates in the Mark and in Pomerania, but who incidentally, like most Brandenburg gentlemen, served their princes in war and sometimes as diplomatists or administrative officials. The record of the family runs back to the thirteenth century, and the estate of Schönhausen has been in its possession for more than three hundred years. On the mother's side Bismarck came of plainer people, but among these also were servants of the state. His maternal grandfather, Menken, was a Prussian government clerk who rose under Frederick William III to the rank of a cabinet councillor and became a trusted assistant of the great Baron Stein.

Social position

The country gentlemen of Prussia held, in Bismarck's youth, a position not unlike that of the landed gentry of England. They were the governing class and managed the affairs of their districts; and the country squire who developed an exceptional talent for administration passed easily and naturally from the government of his neighborhood to the administration of the province or of the

Education

kingdom. By way of preparation for these duties and possibilities, the future landholder sometimes studied law and even entered the judicial or administrative service of the state, without necessarily intending to become either an advocate or a professional official. In accordance with this excellent usage, the young Bismarck, at the age of seventeen, was matriculated in the law faculty at

Göttingen and spent three semesters as a student in that university — but, if Göttingen traditions are to be trusted, can not be said to have studied there. At Berlin, however, where he completed his law course, he must have studied; for he passed the state examination with credit and entered the state service. After one year's work as assistant (*Auscultator*) in the city court of Berlin and nearly three years' administrative service as *Referendar* at Aix-la-Chapelle and Potsdam, he resigned his position and, at the age of twenty-four, assumed with his brother Bernhard the care of his father's Pomeranian estates. For eight years the future chancellor of the German empire devoted himself to sheepraising and grain-growing, relieving the monotony of his life by hard riding and occasional hard drinking, but also by hard reading and travel. In 1845 he was elected a member of the Pomeranian Diet. The death of his father, in the same year, gave him the ancestral seat

Life in the country 1839-47

of Schönhausen and carried him from Pomerania to the Mark. Here he obtained his first administrative office, that of superintendent of dikes; and here also he was elected to the provincial Diet; and when, in 1847, King Frederick William IV attempted to solve the parliamentary question by collecting the representatives of the eight provinces, Bismarck went to Berlin as a member of the United Diet. He was only an alternate delegate; but the proper representative, as it chanced, fell ill, and Bismarck's political career was opened.

Entry into public life

It was an uneasy time in Prussia and in Germany when the United Diet came together, and it was soon to be a stormy time. The German people were dominated by two aspirations, popular sovereignty and national unity. That these objects were not merely distinct but also, under the conditions then existing, incompatible, the people wholly failed to realize. The two ideas had gained their

German politics, 1815-48

hold upon the German mind in the same historic period — that of the first French revolution and the revolutionary wars (1789–1815). The revolution had infected the Germans with the democratic fever, and the subjugation and humiliation of Germany by Napoleon had awakened a specific German patriotism and shown the necessity of national union. In the war of liberation (1813) the German governments, and notably the government of Prussia, had appealed to both of these popular ideas. They had promised the people liberty and unity. When the victory was won, when Napoleon was dethroned and France reduced to its pre-revolutionary boundaries, the German governments broke their pledges. Germany was organized, at the Congress of Vienna (1815), into a loose confederation of sovereign states; and in the majority of these states, including Prussia and Austria, the princes retained absolute power. The people naturally lost all faith in their rulers and began to look to a popular uprising and the establishment of popular sovereignty as the only means of national unification. This connection of ideas determined the creed of both parties. As the nationalists were nearly all Liberals, and to a great extent Democrats, so, by an inevitable antithesis, nearly all the Conservatives were particularists, identifying the maintenance of princely power with the system of state sovereignty and German disunity. All agitation in favor of national unity was punished as treason.

Revolution of March, 1848

The paralysis of princely government in 1848 gave the Liberals an unexpected opportunity to attempt the realization of their programme: unity through liberty. The Paris insurrection and the dethronement of Louis Philippe kindled the flame of revolution throughout Germany; and everywhere, at first, the German revolutionists achieved complete success. All the German princes who had thus far retained absolute power gave or promised constitutions; and those who had already

given constitutions appointed Liberal
ministers and promised Liberal reforms.
Prussia and Austria succumbed to the
popular movement as completely as the
little states; and Austria, the bulwark
of conservatism, was threatened with de-
struction by simultaneous insurrections
in Hungary and Italy. Constitutional
liberty seemed assured, and the Liberal
leaders had for the moment a free field
for their attempt to secure national unity.
A German parliament, elected by universal suffrage, met at Frankfort and
addressed itself to the task of framing
a national constitution for a new German
empire.

Popular unity movement

Frankfort Parliament

It was characteristic of the *doctrinaire*
spirit of the movement that the central
and vital point of the whole question was
the last to be considered. There were
in Germany two great states, either of
which was stronger than all the little
states together; and the prime question
was: Which of these two states, Prussia
or Austria, shall have the hegemony in

Austria or Prussia?

the new Germany? But as neither of these states would peacefully submit to the rule of the other, the question immediately restated itself: Which of these two states is to be excluded from the new Germany? The answer could not be doubtful. Prussia was the more modern and progressive of the two states, and in the customs union it had brought all the German states except Austria into commercial unity. The Parliament finally excluded Austria from the empire, and offered the imperial crown to Frederick William IV of Prussia. But this result was not attained until the spring of 1849. In 1848, when all the petty princes were terrorized by the revolution and the Austrian empire was struggling for existence, the scheme might conceivably have been realized. In 1849 the reaction had begun: the princes had largely recovered their courage and reëstablished their power, and Austria had fought through the worst of its embarrassments. In 1849, there-

Leadership offered to Prussia

fore, the offer of the imperial crown to Frederick William IV was simply an invitation to him to mobilize his army and fight for it. The success of such a venture was doubtful; and from the Conservative point of view the stake was not worth the risk. The Liberals in the Frankfort Parliament had gained the adhesion of the Democrats and secured a majority only by making the constitution of the new empire so democratic that the emperor would have been a mere figurehead. Frederick William of Prussia accordingly refused the imperial crown, and the revolutionary experiment was at an end. The Liberal programme had failed, as in the nature of things it was bound to fail. No confederation has ever been rebuilt into a nation without the cement of blood.

Prussian refusal

For Prussia, however, the recognition of its necessary hegemony by the representatives of the German people had a certain moral value — a value all the greater because the recognition was

Princely movement for unity 1849-50

tardy and reluctant. The Prussian government endeavored to utilize this advantage in 1849 and 1850 by negotiations with the North German princes. A treaty of alliance was concluded with Saxony and Hanover for a "restricted union"; nearly all the lesser states accepted the proposal; and a second Erfurt constituent Parliament met at Erfurt in Parliament the spring of 1850. But the adhesion of Saxony and Hanover was not even half-hearted; there was no heart or sincerity in it. These states were simply temporizing with Prussia. They were really averse to the proposed union and were engaged in simultaneous negotiations with Austria. For a brief space, in 1850, Prussia and Austria seemed likely to come to blows and the German question to a solution. But Russia threw its whole influence and threatened to throw its whole force on the side of Austria; Olmütz and Prussia, in the convention of Olmütz, November 29, 1850, yielded every point in dispute. The old confederation was

reëstablished in all its old impotence,
and the Federal Diet resumed its ses-
sions at Frankfort.

What was Bismarck's position on all
these questions? Towards the constitutional movement in Prussia his attitude
was one of bitter and uncompromising
hostility. In the United Diet of 1847–48
he figured as a Tory of the Tories. He
was more royalist than the king, and
opposed every diminution of the kingly
prerogatives. When in the spring of
1848 the king promised a constitution
and the United Diet passed an address
of thanks, Bismarck was one of the few
who voted against the address. He
accepted the situation, he declared, because he could not help it; but he was
not willing to close his activity in the
Diet with the lying assertion that he
was thankful for what he was obliged to
regard as a mistake. When the king
summoned a representative assembly to
frame the promised constitution, Bis-

Bismarck's
Toryism

marck refused to stand for election.
When the king dissolved this assembly,
published a constitution of his own and
ordered new elections, Bismarck accepted
a mandate as deputy in the new Diet; but
this he did only on the personal solici-
tation of the king.

Attitude
toward
the unity
movements
Toward the popular unity movement
his attitude was that of an unfriendly
critic. He approved the king's refusal
of the imperial title offered by the Frankfort Parliament, because the Frankfort
constitution would make the emperor
"the vassal" of the Radicals. "The
Frankfort crown," Bismarck said, "may
be very brilliant; but the gold which
gives truth to its brilliancy is to be got-
ten by putting the Prussian crown into
the melting pot." Bismarck sat in the
Erfurt Parliament, but he saw clearly the
hopelessness of its attempts and occupied himself in throwing cold water
upon the enthusiasts. During the
Austro-Prussian disputes of 1850 he
voted with the Austrophils in the Prussian

Diet, and defended the convention of Olmütz.

When the German confederation was reëstablished, Frederick William IV sent Bismarck to the Frankfort Diet as the representative of Prussia. This appointment elicited hostile comment. The Frankfort Diet was nothing but a standing congress of ambassadors and the appointment of a man without diplomatic training was a breach of Prussian traditions. Upon the Prussian representative at Frankfort, moreover, rested in large measure the defence of Prussia's German interests, and the appointment of a pronounced friend of Austria seemed likely to result in a sacrifice of these interests. Bismarck undoubtedly owed his appointment to his legitimist, or rather absolutist, attitude in Prussian politics. His defence of the royal prerogative had won him the confidence of the king. His attitude towards Austria made his appointment particularly suitable. After Olmütz, it

Envoy at Frankfort 1851–59

would have been absurd for Prussia to
send to Frankfort an ambassador who was
not *persona grata* to Austria.

Bismarck's appointment was no error.
His attitude towards Austria resulted in
no sacrifice of Prussia's interests. His
support of Austria during his parliamentary career had been dictated by party feeling. The Conservatives rightly regarded
Austria as the bulwark of conservatism,
and Bismarck was a thorough Conservative. At Frankfort, however, he ceased
to be a Conservative and became simply
a Prussian. He found the Austrian influence in the ascendant and saw that this
influence was constantly used to thwart
Prussia's plans and injure Prussia's pros-
pects. Before he had been in Frankfort
a year, the adroitness and the persistence
with which he countered the Austrian
schemes made him *persona ingrata* at
Vienna, and repeated efforts were made in
the following years to secure his recall.

For this period of Bismarck's career we
possess fuller data than for any other,

Change of
views

because the greater part of his Frankfort correspondence, including not merely official despatches but private letters to the Prussian prime minister, has been given to the public. These despatches and letters are of such literary excellence as to make them one of the monuments of classical German prose; of such intrinsic value that no history of the period can be written without consulting them; and they show such breadth of view and keenness of insight as fully to explain the advancement of the writer to the highest position in the Prussian state. The business actually transacted in the Frankfort Diet was petty and unimportant to the last degree; but Frankfort was a central point of European intrigue, and the most vital questions of European politics were touched in Bismarck's despatches. The king and his minister-president, Manteuffel, consulted their representative at Frankfort upon all leading questions of state policy; and his advice seems commonly to have been followed.

This was notably the case during the Crimean war, when France, England and Austria sought to draw Prussia into an attitude of hostility to Russia, and Bismarck convincingly maintained the absence of any Prussian interest in the war and the impolicy of aiding Austria. His Frankfort experiences had caused him to believe that, in the existing condition of European and German affairs, Austria was Prussia's natural enemy. He wrote in 1856:

Hostility to
Austria

> In every century since the time of Charles V, German dualism has settled its relations by an internal war, fought to the finish ; and in the present century also there will be no other way of setting the clock of our development at the right hour. . . . I desire to express my conviction that at no distant time we shall have to fight with Austria for our existence.

And in 1859, just after the outbreak of the Italian war, he wrote that the embarrassments of Austria gave Prussia an exceptional opportunity to readjust its relations to Germany; that these relations amounted, for Prussia, to a disease; and that this disease, unless radically cured at some such favorable moment, would have to be treated, sooner or later, *ferro et igni.* Here is already the line of thought which led to the war of 1866 and the formation of the North German confederation; and here is also, in its first form, the famous phrase *Eisen und Blut.*

In the following year, alluding to rumors of his own leanings toward a French alliance, he wrote to a friend: " If I have sold myself, it is to a Teutonic and not to a Gallic devil"; and in another letter he declared that he could not see why Prussia should shrink so coyly from the idea of a representative German parliament. *A German policy*

The letters last cited were written from St. Petersburg. Bismarck's hostility to Austria had become so pronounced that the Prussian government, not yet prepared to accept his policy, had deemed it advisable to promote him out of Frankfort and, as he himself expressed it, to *Ambassador to Russia 1859–62*

c

"put him on ice" on the Neva. Here he remained as Prussian ambassador for three years.

William 1 (1861-88)
During the latter part of Bismarck's term of service at Frankfort, King Frederick William IV had been attacked by a disease of the brain, and in 1858 his brother, Prince William, had assumed the regency. In 1861 Frederick William died, and the prince regent became king.

Reform of the army
One of the chief causes of Prussia's disgraceful submission at Olmütz was the imperfect condition of its army; and King William, a soldier before all things, was resolved upon a thorough reorganization of "the instrument." The plan

Opposition of the Diet
involved a serious increase of the budget, and this the Chamber of Deputies refused. Foreseeing an obstinate conflict, the king wavered for a time between two courses: abdication or the enforcement of the royal will in spite of the Deputies. If he chose the latter course, he needed as premier a man completely devoted to prerogative,

resolute in action and fearless of consequences; and there was no man among
his subjects who possessed these qualities
in a higher degree than his ambassador
at St. Petersburg. The minister of war,
von Roon, whom the king liked and
trusted above all his advisers and who
was a friend of Bismarck, was persistent
in urging Bismarck's appointment. Early
in 1862 Bismarck was recalled from Russia, apparently with a view to his becom-
ing prime minister; but the king could
not yet make up his mind and Bismarck
was sent to Paris. In the autumn of the
same year von Roon telegraphed: " The
pear is ripe"; and Bismarck returned to
Berlin and was appointed president of the
Prussian ministry.

Contemporary letters and memoirs published in the last few years have made it
clear that at this time (1862) King William neither liked Bismarck nor fully
trusted him. The dislike was caused,
in part, by Bismarck's extreme frankness
and frequent brusqueness of speech; the

Bismarck ambassador to France

Minister-president

William's distrust of Bismarck

distrust was not of Bismarck's ability or loyalty but of his discretion. Under both sentiments lay, as Erich Marcks has shrewdly suggested, the natural antipathy which common sense feels toward genius.

Bismarck was called to the premiership because he undertook to secure the reorganization of the army in spite of the Deputies, and because he convinced the king that this could be done without violating the constitution. It was not William's intention to abandon the personal direction of Prussia's general policy. In fact, however, it was Bismarck's will and not the king's that determined Prussian action from 1862 to 1870 and German action from 1870 to 1888. This result was not reached without friction nor without occasional crises. William possessed too strong a character to accept, without resistance, plans that he only partially comprehended and ventures of which he could not foresee the outcome. He was also,

(marginal note:) Bismarck's management of William

with all his ambition, too conscientious
a man to do what he thought wrong.
Bismarck, however, had a remarkable
power of lucid statement and of coercive
reasoning; and when persuasion failed,
he did not hesitate to break the king's
resistance by the irresistible logic of
events. In many cases William doubtless failed to see that the situation which
constrained him had been deliberately
created by his minister. There can be
little question that in 1866 he as firmly
believed Austria to be the aggressor as
he believed France to be the aggressor
in 1870. To Bismarck, William's re-
luctances were often troublesome; but
they had for Prussia a value which Bismarck did not fail to recognize: they
minimized the impression of unscrupu-
lousness which the minister's policy was
too apt to create.

During the first four years of Bismarck's administration, Prussia's internal
politics were extremely simple although

Parliamen-
tary conflict
1862-66

very stormy. Each year the Deputies
refused to vote the increased military
appropriations. Each year the Diet was
dissolved and new elections ordered.
Each new election increased the anti-
governmental majority. But the people,
even when the agitation was hottest, continued to pay their taxes; and the upper
house, which was completely under the
control of the government, voted the
desired appropriations. The money was
then spent by the government without
authorization from the Deputies, and the
army was reorganized according to the
plans of the king and his minister of
war.

Foreign
policy
1862-66

Prussia's foreign policy during these
years, on the other hand, seems very
intricate and somewhat tortuous; and as
far as the details are concerned it was
necessarily so. Bismarck had assumed
the direction of Prussia's affairs with the
intention of solving the German question
by establishing the hegemony of Prussia.
This could be done only after a suc-

cessful war with Austria. To assure Austria
Prussia's triumph, Austria must remain
isolated, and to that end Prussia must
maintain cordial relations with France
and Russia. So far, all was clear and
simple; but the method by which these
ends were to be attained could not be
determined in advance: it depended necessarily upon the course of events. Bismarck had devoted his three years in St. Russia
Petersburg to cementing the friendly relations already existing between Russia
and Prussia and had obtained assurance
that Russia would not interfere again, as
in 1850, in behalf of Austria. During
his brief mission in France he seems to France
have convinced himself that Napoleon
III would also remain neutral. As president of the ministry, one of his earliest
acts was to conclude a liberal commercial
treaty with France; and the insurrection
of 1863 in Russian Poland enabled him
to render useful aid to the Russian government. The re-opening of the Schleswig-Holstein question, in the same year,

touched Germany more nearly; and this question, as Bismarck handled it, led directly to the solution of the German problem.

Schleswig-
Holstein
question The Schleswig-Holstein question, although a complicated one, is not so unintelligible as is commonly supposed. These two German duchies had long been united with Denmark; but they were not parts of Denmark, for the union was purely personal: it resulted from the fact that their dukes had become kings of Denmark. The Danes naturally desired to make the union a real one. In the way of their ambition stood the facts that Holstein belonged to the German confederation and that old treaties guaranteed that Schleswig and Holstein should never be separated. Hence the incorporation of Schleswig was impossible without the simultaneous incorporation of Holstein, and the incorporation of Holstein was impossible without the assent of Germany —an assent which the Danes could not

hope to obtain.   This complicated state of
things had already caused much trouble.   In
the revolutionary year of 1848 the Schleswig-Holsteiners had risen against the
Danes and attempted to establish their
independence, and Germany had actively
supported the movement.   But when the
German revolution was suppressed, the
Schleswig-Holstein revolution shared its
fate.   The revolt of the duchies was regarded by the Conservatives generally,
and by the governments of Austria and
Prussia in particular, simply as an insurrection against constituted princely authority; and both Prussia and Austria
aided in the restoration of the duchies to
their lawful sovereign.   The whole question
of their relation to Denmark, present and
future, was discussed in London in 1852,
and an attempt was made to settle it by
a European treaty.   It was then already
foreseen that the union with Denmark,
established by a dynastic accident, was
likely to be severed in the same way.
The main line of the ruling dynasty was

Revolt of
the duchies
1848

London
conference
1852

dying out; and the succession to the
Danish throne was certain to pass, sooner
or later, to the Glücksburg branch of
the family. But this branch derived title
through the female line, and the succession in Schleswig-Holstein was gov-
erned by the Salic law. Schleswig-
Holstein accordingly would pass, not to
the Glücksburg, but to the younger Augustenburg line. The London conference
undertook to change all this. It decreed
that Schleswig-Holstein should be permanently associated with Denmark, and
that the succession, both in Denmark
and in the duchies, should be vested in
the Glücksburg heirs. This treaty or
protocol of May 8, 1852, was signed
by Prussia and Austria as European
powers; but it was not ratified by the
German confederation nor in any way
accepted by the Schleswig-Holsteiners.
And the Prussian and Austrian ambassadors signed the London protocol only
after, and in consideration of, a previous
treaty with Denmark, by which that

London
protocol
1852

kingdom bound itself to respect the autonomy of the Schleswig-Holsteiners and not to incorporate Schleswig.

Such was the position of affairs when King Frederick VII of Denmark issued a decree (the patent of March 30, 1863) which separated Schleswig from Holstein and practically incorporated the former in the kingdom of Denmark. The German powers at once protested; and the Federal Diet, in October, ordered an "execution" in Holstein, *i. e.* voted to send troops there. On November 14 a new Danish parliament, representing Denmark and Schleswig, voted a new constitution incorporating Schleswig. On the following day Frederick VII died. His successor, Christian IX, signed the new constitution. Frederick's death complicated the question of the special rights of Schleswig with the broader question of the succession in both duchies. By the London protocol Christian IX became duke of Schleswig-Holstein as well as king of Denmark. But the

Danish aggression 1863

Death of the Danish king

Dispute over the succession

German confederation, as we have seen, had never agreed to this, nor had the Schleswig-Holsteiners. In their opinion Christian of Glücksburg had no rights in the duchies; and when, in December, the federal execution was carried into effect by an army of 12,000 Saxons and Hanoverians, Frederick of Augustenburg was acclaimed as duke, and took up his residence at Kiel.

Prussia's choice of courses in 1863

To the Prussian government two courses were open. It could recognize the London protocol as still in force and compel Christian IX, as duke of Schleswig-Holstein, to observe the preliminary treaty which guaranteed Schleswig's autonomy;

The popular course

or it could declare the London protocol abrogated, recognize Frederick of Augustenburg as duke and help him to gain possession of Schleswig. The public sentiment of Prussia, as of the other German states, was strongly in favor of the latter course. By adopting it Bismarck would at once have become the popular leader

of a national movement, but he would
have imperilled the real interests not only
of Prussia but also of Germany. The
revolutionary character of the popular
programme and the violation of treaties
which it required would have aroused the
opposition of Europe. Prussia and the
German patriots would have stood alone
together, as in 1850; and, if successful
against such odds, they would simply
have added a new petty sovereignty to a
Germany cursed already with over-many
sovereignties. If, on the other hand, the   The
Prussian government should accept the   unpopular
course
situation created by the treaties of 1852,
it could indeed demand that Schleswig
be not incorporated in Denmark, but
if this point should be conceded, Prussia
would be obliged to restore both duchies
to their Danish ruler. This was what
Austria desired and the German patriots
dreaded. Bismarck, however, had satisfied
himself that the party in power at Copen-
hagen would accept war rather than give
up the incorporation of Schleswig; and

war once declared, he foresaw that the prize of victory would be whatever the

victor chose to make it. The Prussian cabinet accordingly announced that it recognized the treaties of 1852 as binding, and that it demanded from Denmark nothing but the observance of those treaties — a declaration in which Austria gladly joined. The storm of protest which this action aroused in the Prussian Diet and throughout Germany was used by Bismarck to secure Austria's support in decisive measures against Denmark, and to avert the intervention of the other European powers. "If you do not support the moderate measures which we deem necessary," Bismarck said to Austria, — "If you oppose the just and temperate course which we are pursuing," he declared to the other powers, — "my colleagues and I will retire from the ministry. The king will then be forced to summon into power the leaders of the German revolutionary party." For fear of worse things Austria went hand in hand with

Prussia, and Europe looked on inactive.
The Danes, as Bismarck expected, refused to abrogate their new constitution,
and war was declared. In February, 1864,   War with
                                             Denmark
an army of 60,000 Austrians and Prus-   1864
sians invaded Schleswig, and on April 18
the Prussians stormed the redoubts of
Düppel. A week later representatives
of the European powers met in London,
agreed upon an armistice and endeavored
to negotiate a treaty of peace. The negotiations were fruitless. The Danes still
refused to reëstablish the personal union
and demanded the annexation of a portion at least of Schleswig. The war was
renewed, the allies were victorious, and by
the treaty of Vienna, October 30, 1864,
Denmark ceded Schleswig-Holstein and
the little duchy of Lauenburg to Prussia
and Austria.

This *condominium* or joint sovereignty   *Condominium*
of Prussia and Austria in the duchies   in Schleswig-
                                            Holstein
was precisely what Bismarck desired.   1864-66
Believing that war with Austria was

necessary for the solution of the German
question, it seemed to him convenient ͵
to have a cause of war always ready;
and such a relation as that now established in the duchies would necessarily be
fruitful of causes for war. Further, whenever the war should come, these duchies
would be for Prussia an extremely desirable addition to the stake in play. They
represented a possible gain for Prussia, but
no possible gain for Austria. Their position would make their annexation to
Prussia both feasible and natural, while
Austria could in no case dream of annexing
them. From this point of view, Bismarck's
diplomacy was especially skilful, and the
association of Austria in the enterprise
was its most masterly feature. Bismarck
himself declared, after the French war,
that the Schleswig-Holstein campaign
was the one of which, from a political
point of view, he was proudest.

How Aus-
tria's play
was forced
It has often been asked, in the light
of subsequent events, why Austria joined
forces with Prussia. It is difficult to see

how Austria could have acted otherwise.
If Bismarck had repudiated the London
treaties, then indeed Austria's course
would have been clear. It could have
put itself at the head of a European
concert for the restraint and punishment
of the Prussian law-breakers. Bismarck,
however, assumed an attitude of unimpeach-
able legality, which was also in consonance
with the Austro-Prussian policy of 1850;
and Austria was compelled either to act
with Prussia or not to act at all. Austrian neutrality, however, would have
left Prussia in complete control of the
field. Prussia would have made war
alone; would have annexed the duchies
at its close; would have gained greatly
in power and enormously in prestige.
This Austria could not tolerate; and
unless it were prepared, as Bismarck had
already suggested, to " transfer its centre
of gravity to Ofen," it had to go with
Prussia in order to see that Prussia did
not go too far. It cannot be maintained
that Austria was duped; for when, at

D

an early stage of the joint action, the Austrian cabinet attempted to stipulate that the duchies should be restored to Denmark unless both powers agreed upon some other disposition, Bismarck refused his assent and substituted a stipulation, which the Austrian ministry accepted, that the eventual disposition of the duchies should be determined by agreement between the two contracting powers.

Strained relations with Austria

The joint ownership of the duchies speedily led, as Bismarck had anticipated, to dissension. Austria was willing to turn them over to Prussia in return for compensation in Silesia. King William, however, refused to cede any portion of Silesia. Austria then espoused the cause of the Augustenburg prince. Prussia protested, and war seemed imminent in 1865. It was postponed, not so much by Bismarck's will as by the king's, and a temporary adjustment was reached in the

Convention of Gastein 1865

convention of Gastein. By this treaty Prussia bought out Austria's rights in

Lauenburg, and the administration of government in the two other duchies was divided, Prussia assuming control of Schleswig and Austria of Holstein. But the truce was a short one. Prussia accused Austria of encouraging the Augustenburg agitation, and when, on June 1, 1866, Austria submitted the Schleswig-Holstein question to the Federal Diet, Prussia declared the treaty of Gastein broken and the joint administration of the duchies reëstablished. Prussian troops were accordingly sent into Holstein. Austria pronounced this a breach of the peace; and on June 11 the Austrian representative in the Federal Diet proposed the mobilization against Prussia of the contingents of all the other German states. This motion was carried, June 14, by a three-fifths vote. The Prussian representative declared, in the name of his government, that this attempt to levy federal war upon a member of the confederation was a breach of the fundamental pact of union, and that the con-

New dissensions

federation was thereby dissolved. He added that it was the purpose of his government to find for the unity of the German people a form better suited to the conditions of the age.

The German question

For nearly three months, in accordance with a plan foreshadowed in his earlier letters, Bismarck had been pushing the German question to the front. He had been agitating, by circulars to all the German governments, the question of federal reform, and on April 9 he had caused a proposal to be introduced in the Federal Diet for the establishment of a German parliament on the basis of manhood suffrage. Immediately after the vote of June 14, Prussia called upon the governments of Saxony, Hanover and Hesse-Cassel to join in the establishment of a new federal union. Upon their refusal Prussian troops invaded these territories, and the war for the control of Germany began on June 16, 1866.

The war with Austria, 1866

Neither Austria nor Prussia stood alone. Austria was supported by all the South

German states, *viz.* Bavaria, Würtemberg,
Baden and Hesse-Darmstadt, and by the
more important states of North Germany,
viz. Hanover, Saxony, Hesse-Cassel and
Nassau. Prussia had secured the alliance
of Italy by a secret treaty (April 8). In
case of victory Italy was to receive
Venice. The war was practically terminated by the great Prussian victory of
Königgrätz or Sadowa, July 3. After   Sadowa
Sadowa, Prussia was in a position to dic-
tate the terms of peace. The military
men wished to enter Vienna and to demand a strip of Bohemian territory. Bismarck feared a joint intervention of the
neutral powers and desired a speedy set-
tlement. He also urged the impolicy of
inflicting lasting wounds upon Austria's
national pride; and after a hard struggle
he carried his point. Preliminaries of   Peace of
peace were signed at Nicolsburg, July 26,   Prague
and the final treaty at Prague, August 23.
Italy received Venice; Austria conveyed
to Prussia its interests in Schleswig-
Holstein and recognized the dissolution

of the old German confederation and the creation of a new North German confederation, to be composed of the states north of the Main. North of the Main, also, Prussia was to annex such territories as it saw fit, promising to spare Saxony. The South German states were to be permitted to form an independent confederation of their own. Austria was for ever excluded from Germany.

Napoleon's interference

To these arrangements Napoleon III was in fact though not ostensibly a party. It was French influence, backed by the prospect of French intervention, that secured the recognition of South German independence. In consideration of the abandonment — or rather postponement — of Prussian hegemony over South Germany, Napoleon assented to more extensive Prussian annexations in North Germany than were at first proposed.

Prussian annexations

Prussia annexed Schleswig-Holstein, Hanover, Hesse-Cassel, Nassau and the free city of Frankfort, adding four and a half millions to its population and in-

creasing its territory by a fourth. The
annexation of Hanover was especially ad-
vantageous; it rounded out what Motley
had described as " Prussia's wasp-waist."

All the rest of the German states north
of the Main, including the kingdom of
Saxony, ten duchies, seven principalities,
and the free cities of Hamburg, Lübeck
and Bremen, joined with Prussia in the
formation of a new federal union — the
North German confederation. Its constitution was draughted by Bismarck, accepted by the governments of the single
states, and submitted in 18 to an Imperial Diet chosen by manhood suffrage.
After this Diet had passed it with a
number of amendments, it was ratified
without further amendment by the leg-
islatures of the single states. Under its
provisions the executive powers of the
union were vested in a president (the
king of Prussia) and a Federal Council consisting of appointed representatives
of the different states. In this council
Prussia was to have seventeen votes, Saxony

The North German con-federation

four, the larger duchies and principalities each three or two, and the smaller principalities and the free cities each one. The presidency of the council was entrusted to a chancellor, appointed by the federal president. (Bismarck, of course, became chancellor.) The legislative power was vested in the Federal Council and an Imperial Diet elected by manhood suffrage. In name federal, the new union was essentially national. Its power extended over military and naval matters; over commerce, railways, telegraphs and the post; over the entire field of judicial organization, criminal law and procedure, civil procedure and commercial law. The change from the old confederation (1815–1866) to this new union was greater than the change from the American articles of confederation to the American constitution of 1789.

In the light of these splendid achievements, the public judgment of Bismarck underwent an immediate and complete

Character of the new union.

reversal. A few of his opponents had been converted to his support by the outcome of the Danish campaign, but until the autumn of 1866 he was generally regarded as a reactionary, pure and simple. His conflict with the Prussian Chamber of Deputies had naturally intensified this impression. In his support of the army reform, in his hostility to the insurgent Poles, in his treatment of the Schleswig-Holstein question, he had defiantly antagonized German public opinion; and when it became evident that his conduct of Prussian policy was certain to produce war with Austria, he was the best hated and the best denounced man in Germany. On May 7, 1866, he narrowly escaped death at the hands of a fanatic named Cohen. The assassin killed himself in prison. Crowds of people visited the cell, and women covered Cohen's body with flowers and crowns of laurel.

The revulsion of feeling which followed the Austrian war, and the sudden popularity of its author, were not due solely, nor even chiefly, to the vulgar admiration of success. Bismarck had realized the deepest desire of the German people. He had made Germany a nation, with a legislature resting on the broadest and most popular basis. He also made peace with the Prussian Chamber of Deputies. To the dismay of his Tory supporters, and not without a struggle with his royal master, he asked and received indemnity for governing without a budget, thus recognizing the rights of the Chamber and the abnormal character of his own administration during the period of conflict. The natural result was a complete disorganization of the parliamentary opposition and a general shifting of party lines. The best elements of the opposition, the Old Liberals of 1848, formed a new National Liberal group, which during the next ten years generally acted in concert with the government and, with the Conservatives, gave it a working majority both in the Prussian Diet and in the Imperial Parliament.

Bill of indemnity

Shifting of party lines

This simplified the internal politics of Prussia and of the confederation; but the foreign relations of the new union were far from satisfactory. Napoleon, as we have seen, had thus far shown himself friendly to Prussia. He had intimated, in 1865, his willingness to conclude an offensive alliance against Austria (Prussia to reorganize Germany and France to receive payment on the left bank of the Rhine); and in spite of the rejection of this offer he had actively furthered the conclusion of the alliance between Prussia and Italy. He did not believe that Prussia was a match for Austria; he believed that his aid would still be needed, and that he would ultimately get his price. Sadowa defeated these schemes; and after Sadowa he should have seen that nothing was to be gained by negotiation. He could not or would not see this, and at once began to demand compensation for his neutrality. At Nicolsburg, in July, 1866, his ambassador, M. Benedetti, demanded a rectification of France's east-

Strained relations with France

Compensations demanded

ern frontier. On August 5 the French demands were put into definite form. Prussia was to grant France the frontier of 1814, and was to obtain from Bavaria and from Hesse-Darmstadt the cession of their provinces on the left bank of the Rhine. Luxemburg was to be separated from Germany and the Prussian garrison was to be withdrawn from the fortress.[1] Bismarck promptly declared that the cession of German territory could not be considered. On August 20 Benedetti declared that France would be satisfied with Saarlouis, Landau and Luxemburg; but if Prussia would help France to acquire

[1] Luxemburg belonged, at this time, to the king of the Netherlands. It had formed part of the old German confederation. The fortress of Luxemburg was a federal fortress, and the Prussian garrison was stationed there in accordance with federal treaty. With the dissolution of the old confederation, Luxemburg was already practically separated from Germany, and the reason for keeping a Prussian garrison in the fortress had disappeared. Napoleon desired that Prussia should recognize these facts and inferences, in order that the way might be clear for his acquiring Luxemburg from the king of the Netherlands.

Belgium, France would permit Prussia
to incorporate South Germany in the
German confederation.   On August 29, Evidence of
French
demands
secured
Benedetti put this latter suggestion into
the form of a draught treaty in his own
handwriting.   It has never been shown
that Bismarck agreed to any of these
demands; but he undoubtedly permitted
the French ambassador to hope that some
compensation would be conceded. " Au
moins," as Sorel neatly says, "il y avait eu
dialogue"; and it is inconceivable that
Benedetti should have gone so far without
considerable encouragement.   Bismarck
has himself admitted that he pursued a
" dilatory " policy.   His object was twofold.
He desired to postpone the inevitable war
with France until the Prussian military
system was introduced in the annexed
provinces and in the other German states;
and he desired documentary evidence of
the French demands.   This, as we have
seen, he obtained; and of the documents Use made of
the evidence
thus obtained he made very effective use.
During the peace negotiations between

Prussia and Bavaria in August, 1866, Bavaria appealed to Napoleon for his good offices, which Napoleon promptly granted. Bismarck met this move by exhibiting to the Bavarian minister the draught treaty of August 5, showing him that his friend the emperor of the French had asked Prussia for large portions of Bavarian and Hessian territory. The result of this revelation was the immediate conclusion, not merely of a treaty of peace, but also of a secret treaty of offensive and defensive alliance between Prussia and Bavaria (August 22). Similar treaties had already been concluded with Würtemberg and Baden. Equally effective use was made of the draught treaty concerning Belgium. It was published in the London *Times* of July 25, 1870, a few days after the French declaration of war. The effect of this disclosure upon the public opinion of England and of Europe was all that Bismarck could desire.

The prime cause of the Franco-German war was the irritation felt by the French people at the growth of a first-class power on their eastern frontier. A long step had been taken in 1866 towards German unity, and the completion of this movement, it was felt, would threaten the traditional primacy of France in Europe. A secondary cause was the failure of the French government to obtain territorial compensation for the increased power of Prussia. After the unsuccessful negotiations described above, Napoleon attempted in 1867 to carry out a part at least of his programme by purchasing Luxemburg from the king of the Netherlands. This attempt created great indignation among the people of Germany; and the military party at Berlin, believing that a contest with France was inevitable, wished to precipitate the war before the French army reforms, then under discussion, were completed. Bismarck, however, declared that "the personal conviction of a ruler or statesman, however well

Genesis of the Franco-German war

Luxemburg incident 1867

founded, that war will eventually break out, cannot justify its promotion." He contrived to defeat the purchase of Luxemburg without giving the French government any tangible grievance against Prussia. But Napoleon felt that he had again been duped, and the incident increased the tension between the two nations. A large body of Napoleon's warmest supporters began to agitate for war against Prussia as the only means of rehabilitating the prestige of the dynasty.

Coalition against Germany

Negotiations were opened by Napoleon with the emperor of Austria and the king of Italy for joint action against Prussia; and although, because of the failure of the three courts to reach any satisfactory agreement on the Roman question, no formal treaty was signed, an understanding was attained early in June, 1870, that if France declared war upon Prussia and succeeded in occupying South Germany, then Austria and Italy, having gained time for mobilization by a temporary neutrality, would also declare war and add their forces to those of France. War, it appears, was not contemplated before 1871, for the Austrian military authorities stipulated that the declaration of war by France should be made not later than in April.

The immediate occasion of the war was the Spanish candidacy of Prince Leopold of Hohenzollern. This prince, although a Hohenzollern, was not a member of the Prussian royal house but of the South German and Catholic house of Hohenzollern-Sigmaringen. He was more closely connected with the imperial family of France than with the royal family of Prussia. By family compact, however, the king of Prussia was recognized as the head of the house. The Spanish ministry, in search of a Catholic king, had repeatedly offered to present Leopold's name to the Cortes — twice in 1869 and again in March, 1870 — but the offer had been declined. King William advised against the acceptance of the candidacy, and in 1869 Bismarck was of

The Spanish candidacy

E.

the same mind. In 1870, however, Bismarck advised acceptance. His change
of opinion, he said, was due to the fact
that the Spanish revolutionary government, unstable in 1869, had obtained in
1870 the complete control of the country. When the third offer had been declined, Bismarck secured, through Prussian agents, a fourth offer; and in June,
1870, largely in consequence of his advice, Leopold consented to become a candidate. King William was informed of
the prince's decision and declared that he
could interpose no objection. Although
these negotiations were conducted quietly,
they were not kept secret from Napoleon. In the interest of his dynasty, the
emperor would probably have preferred
Leopold to the Orleanist duke de Mont-
pensier, who was, in 1870, the only other
prominent candidate; but he had informed Benedetti, and Benedetti had
probably informed Bismarck, that the
French people would not tolerate a
Hohenzollern candidacy. German writ-

ers assert, however, that Bismarck did not expect serious opposition from Napoleon; and, as a further proof of his pacific intentions, they point out that he had kept open a line of retreat. This latter assertion is true. Bismarck had caused the question to be dealt with from the outset as one that in no wise concerned the Prussian state, and that concerned the king only as titular head of the Sigmaringen branch of the family. From this point of view, Leopold's acceptance concerned only himself and Spain; and the same would be true of his withdrawal. It would in no wise compromise the dignity or lessen the prestige of Prussia. The other assertion, however, that Bismarck expected no serious opposition on Napoleon's part, is far from plausible. The facts seem to be that Bismarck promoted the candidacy with the expectation that opposition would be encountered, and planned at the same time that his candidate should withdraw when the opposition had become manifest.

What were his motives? In the present state of our information, only a con-
jectural answer is possible. If we assume
that Bismarck was aware of the arrangements that were making for an attack
on Germany in 1871, we can see why he
should desire to provoke a declaration
of war in 1870 before those arrangements
were perfected. He would naturally
desire, further, that France should declare war under such circumstances that
European public opinion would condemn
its action. Prince Leopold's candidacy
would not give France a very good *casus
belli;* and if by any chance France
should declare war after Prince Leopold's
withdrawal, the situation, from the German point of view, would be ideal. It
is perhaps improbable that Bismarck's
calculations had been pushed to this
point in the spring of 1870; but he must
have foreseen that Prince Leopold's acceptance and withdrawal would place
Napoleon and his ministers in a difficult position—a position in which it

would be easy to blunder; and we know
that he had little respect for Napoleon's
capacity and still less for that of de Gramont, the new French minister of foreign affairs. He had long since described
Napoleon as *une grande incapacité mé-
connue*, and he had declared that Gramont
was the greatest blockhead (*Dummkopf*)
in Europe.

When, early in July, the news of the
prince's acceptance reached Paris by way
of Madrid, great indignation was mani-
fested in the French journals and by the
French government. Gramont declared
the candidacy an attempt " to reëstablish
the empire of Charles V." A protest
sent to Berlin elicited from an under-
secretary (Bismarck was in Varzin) the
information that Prussia had nothing to
do with the candidacy. Benedetti was
then instructed to proceed to Ems, where
King William was taking the waters, and
to ask the king to obtain from Prince
Leopold a withdrawal of his acceptance.
The king answered that he had no right

Leopold's acceptance

French demand

William's
attitude to address such a demand to the prince;
but he told Benedetti that if the prince
saw fit to withdraw he would approve the
withdrawal. On July 12 the French
government received notice, again from
Leopold's
withdrawal Madrid, that Prince Leopold's acceptance
had been withdrawn. This was regarded
throughout Europe as the end of the
incident. It was felt that the French
government had carried its point and
that there would be no war. Napoleon
and his prime minister, Ollivier, expressed
themselves in this sense. Bismarck, who
had reached Berlin and had intended to
proceed at once to Ems, decided to stay
in Berlin. But Gramont, supported in
this by the general feeling of Paris and
of the Deputies, declared that the satisfaction obtained by France was inade-
New French
demands quate. He suggested to Werther, the
Prussian ambassador, that King William
should write an explanatory letter to the
emperor; and, with Napoleon's assent, he
instructed Benedetti to obtain from the
king an assurance that the candidacy

would not be renewed. On the morning of July 13 the king was asked to give such a pledge, and refused. He told Benedetti that this demand indicated to him a determination on the part of the French government to force a war. In the French cabinet, on the evening of the 13th, it was not felt that the king's refusal made war necessary. Energetic remonstrances from the representatives of friendly powers had convinced Napoleon and his ministers that they had gone too far, and their feeling was in favor of accepting the situation. On the 14th, in consequence of action taken by Bismarck the day before, they decided upon war; and on the 15th war was declared.

France disposed to retreat

On the morning of the 13th, as soon as he heard of the new French demands of the 12th, Bismarck for the first time took an active part in the controversy. He explained to the English ambassador that France was obviously determined on war, and that it was now Prussia's turn to demand explanations and assurances. He

Bismarck intervenes

notified Werther that his conduct in en-
tertaining the demand for " a letter of
apology " was disapproved, and directed
him to take leave of absence on account
of ill health. On the evening of the same
day he received a telegraphic account of
the occurrences of the morning at Ems,
closing with the suggestion, on the part
of the king, that the new French demand
and its refusal be made public. This

"Editing" suggestion Bismarck carried out in the
the Ems
despatch most literal fashion, omitting all details.
The account thus given to the public created the impression that the negotiations
in Ems had terminated more abruptly

Effect of than was really the case. The Germans
Bismarck's
action thought that King William had been
insulted,— which was true, as regarded the
substance of the French demand, but un-
true as regarded the form of its presentation,— and the smouldering indignation
that had been kindled by the arrogant
tone of the French orators and of the
French press burst into a flame of wrath.
The Parisians thought that their ambas-

sador had been insulted, and demanded an immediate declaration of war. Napoleon and his ministers knew that Benedetti's dismissal had been courteous; but they saw that peace could be preserved only by an obvious and unmistakable retreat, on their part, from the ill-considered position which they had taken on July 12. Bismarck had so utilized their mistake as to hold them to its consequences.

The way in which the French ministers handled the Hohenzollern candidacy
shows that they regarded it, at the outset, as a favorable issue on which to force
a war. If France should declare war on a
distinctly German question, all Germany,
they foresaw, would side with Prussia, and
it would be difficult for Austria to inter-
vene. By selecting a question which concerned only the Prussian dynasty they
hoped to secure the neutrality of the
South German states and the active as-
sistance of Austria. When, after being
deprived of their original grievance, they

French
expectations ▾

nevertheless declared war, they undoubtedly hoped that the French troops would
secure, without serious opposition, the
control of South Germany before the
North German mobilization was completed, and that Austria and Italy, in
spite of the lateness of the season, would
come to their aid. These hopes proved
Attitude of futile. In South Germany, as in the
South North, the war was regarded as an
Germany attack on German independence, and
the South German states at once placed
their armies at the disposal of the king
of Prussia. The North German troops
were concentrated on the Alsacian frontier with unexpected rapidity, while the
French mobilization proved far slower
than was anticipated. From the start
France was thrown on the defensive.
Partly for this reason, partly because held
in check by Russia, Austria remained
neutral. The king of Italy, in spite of
the dissent of his ministers, desired to
come to Napoleon's aid; but the success of the Prussian arms was too rapid

and complete to encourage interference. Seven weeks after the declaration of war the entire force with which Napoleon took the field was destroyed, captured or shut up in besieged fortresses. After Sedan the issue of the struggle was certain ; but the heroic obstinacy of the French people prolonged the war for six months. Preliminaries of peace were signed at Versailles, February 26, and the final treaty at Frankfort, May 10, 1871. France ceded to Germany Alsace, including Strasburg, and part of Lorraine, including Metz, — about 1,500,000 souls, — and agreed to pay a war indemnity of 5,000,000,000 francs.

German victories

Peace of Frankfort

The most important result of this war was the completion of German unity. In South Germany local patriotism and religious prejudice had heretofore stood in the way of union with Prussia. These obstacles were swept away in the enthusiasm of this national war. In the march from the Rhine to the Seine, Bavarians,

The German empire

Würtembergers, Hessians and Prussians felt themselves, as never before, one great people. The diplomatists had only to put the stamp of law upon the accomplished fact. During the winter treaties of union were concluded between the North German confederation and the South German states; and on January 18, in the hall of mirrors in Versailles, King William was proclaimed German emperor. The prophecy of Frederick William IV had come true — that the imperial crown would be won on the field of battle.

The new empire, with its twenty-five states and its one territory (Alsace-Lorraine), embraced, at its establishment, over 40,000,000 people, a number which has since risen, by the natural increase of population and in spite of emigration, to more than 53,000,000. Its constitution is simply a revised edition of the North German constitution of 1867. The position of the South German states, barring a few reserved rights, is identical with that of the North German states. Their governments are represented in the Federal Council and their people in the Imperial Diet.

In this parliament Bismarck never found — nor in the light of his experience with the Prussian Diet could he have hoped to create — a passive instrument of his or the emperor's will. The parliament and the people behind it have always had and have constantly asserted an independent will of their own. But the people and the parliament of the new empire have not at any time offered any such blind and obstinate resistance to the realization of vital national interests as did the Prussian deputies before 1866. The internal politics of the empire have been full of conflict; but every conflict has been fought out within the lines of the constitution, and settled by some compromise which has preserved at once the interests of the state and the liberties of the citizen.

The German parliament 1871-90

The Centrists   The most powerful and the most troublesome element of opposition was the
Ultramontane or Centre party, which had
sixty-three votes in the first parliament of
the empire (1871–74), and since 1874 has
regularly numbered about one hundred
— a little more than a fourth of the entire membership. It was ostensibly established to defend the liberties of the
Roman Catholic church in Germany;
but it was established at a time when
no measure menacing those liberties had
been passed or even proposed. It really
represented, in the first place, the hostility of the Roman curia to the establishment in central Europe of a powerful
empire with a Protestant head; and it
embodied, in the second place, a great
deal of the local disaffection due to the
annexations of 1866. Its leader, Windthorst, was formerly a minister of the
king of Hanover; and the malcontent
Hanoverians (Guelphs) have regularly
acted and voted as its allies. The out-
spoken disloyalty of some of its mem-

bers and the systematic agitation of the
Jesuits and of a portion of the regular
Catholic clergy induced the imperial and
state governments, first, to adopt repressive measures, and finally to attempt by
law a more exact definition of the limits
of religious liberty. Thus arose the so-
called "culture conflict." Bismarck always objected to this phrase, insisting on
the essentially political character of the
struggle and declaring that, as minister-
president and chancellor, he was not
fighting for culture but for the political interests of the Prussian state and
the German empire. In the main the
conflict was fought out in Prussia and
the other single states, religious affairs
not falling within the imperial jurisdic-
tion. The resistance of the Catholic
clergy to the new laws — particularly to
the Prussian "May laws" of 1873 — was
very bitter and obstinate. In Prussia
nearly all the Catholic bishops were im-
prisoned or expelled; and an alarming
number of parishes were deprived of all

"Culture
conflict"

The May
laws, 1873

spiritual care. The Prussian government soon found itself obliged to ask the Diet for large powers of indulgence and dispensation: in other words, for power to execute the laws or leave them unexecuted at its discretion. The death of Pius IX, January 7, 1878, and the election of a less combative and more politic successor, Leo XIII, facilitated the attainment of a *modus vivendi;* and the disruption of the National Liberal party in 1879 and the resultant disappearance of the governmental majority caused Bismarck to desire a truce. He needed Centrist support; and he secured it on the *do ut des* plan, sacrificing the anticlerical legislation bit by bit in return for votes for governmental measures. A

Close of the conflict, 1887

peace — or rather an indefinite truce — was concluded with the Roman curia in 1887. Prussia had already "revised" the greater portion of its church laws out of existence, and the Pope agreed that the government should be notified of all intended appointments to ecclesiastical offices. But, notwithstanding this arrangement, the Centre maintained its organization and its attitude of general opposition, and Bismarck continued to traffic with its leaders whenever its support was necessary. At the time of his dismissal the governmental reserve of possible concessions was not yet exhausted; there was still enough anti-clerical legislation on the statute-books to carry his successor through one rather difficult legislative period.

The uses of adversity

During this struggle with the church, Bismarck a second time narrowly escaped assassination. On July 13, 1874, while driving in an open carriage, he was shot at by a cooper named Kullmann. At the moment the shot was fired Bismarck had touched his hat in answer to the salutation of an acquaintance, and the ball passed between his temple and wrist. Kullmann assigned the wrongs of the church as the reason for his act.

Second attempt on Bismarck's life, 1874

Much less powerful in parliament, but far more dangerous to the social and political order of the German empire, is the Social Democratic party. The great strength of this party in Germany — in the election of 1890 it cast nearly eleven per cent of the total vote[1] — is partly due to the idealistic character of the German mind, but mainly to the sudden passage of the German people from a system of economic restraint to an almost perfect economic liberty. This change was accomplished by a series of liberal laws enacted by the North German and Imperial Diets, abolishing nearly all restrictions upon trade and industry and giving the laborer full freedom, but exposing him also to the unchecked influence of free competition. All such transitions are of course accompanied by much suffering and discontent; and the discontent of the German

[1] In 1898 the Social Democrats cast nearly 28 per cent of the total vote and carried about one-seventh of the seats in the Imperial Diet.

workingmen found expression in the
Social Democratic movement. The rapid
growth of the party, and the increas-
ingly revolutionary tendency shown in
the speeches and writings of its leaders,
had already caused the imperial and
state governments to consider the
desirability of repressive legislation, Repressive legislation
when, on May 11, 1878, a workingman
named Hödel, who was shown to be
connected with the Social Democrats,
attempted the life of the emperor. Bismarck at once introduced in the Imperial Diet an anti-socialist bill of great
severity, intended to suppress entirely
the spread of Social Democratic doc-
trines. To the majority of the Deputies
the bill seemed too great an invasion of
the freedom of assembly and of the press,
and its passage in the form desired
by the government was refused. On
June 2, a second attempt was made
upon the emperor's life by a man of
university education, Dr. Nobiling. The
emperor was seriously injured, and for a

time his life was thought to be in danger. Bismarck promptly dissolved the parliament and ordered new elections. The electors supported the government, and the new parliament passed the desired measures against the socialists. The law was passed for a term of years only, but was repeatedly reënacted and remained in force until 1890. Bismarck, however, was not satisfied with repressive measures. He believed it necessary

Reform legislation

to strike at the root of the trouble, not, as many Conservatives desired, by abandoning the principles of economic liberty, but by bettering the position of the workingmen. In accordance with this desire, and largely through his influence, rigid employers' liability laws were adopted, and also a remarkable series of statutes organizing a system of compulsory insurance of laborers against accident, disease and old age.

The German army

During these years of conflict with the Ultramontanes and with the Social

Democrats, Bismarck was occupied with
questions even more vital to the new
empire — questions that touched the central points of political power, the army
and the treasury. It was the Prussian
army that had made Germany a nation,
and the maintenance of German unity
was felt to depend upon the strength
and efficiency of the federal army. The
constitution of the empire provides that
every adult German shall be held to
military service, but leaves the details
of army organization to be regulated by
law. The Conservatives desired that this
should be done by an ordinary law, not
limited as to duration; while the Radicals were disposed to demand an annual
regulation. As against the Radical demand, the military authorities insisted
that so complex a machine as the German army could not be run from year
to year with annual risk of parliamentary
interference. Bismarck himself did not
desire a permanent law, because such a
law, he thought, would make any future

increase of the army difficult.   His attitude facilitated a compromise, *viz.* the
periodical passage of laws fixing the
strength of the peace footing for a term
of years.   From the outset, the term
selected was seven years; and at the close
of each septennate the strength of the
army has been increased.   In 1887 the
Diet attempted to shorten the period to
three years.   Bismarck declared this an
attempt to make the federal army "a
parliamentary army," dissolved the Diet,
January 14, 1887, and appealed to the
country.   The country supported the government, returning a Diet in which the
Radical faction lost two-thirds of its
strength; and the new parliament voted a
new septennate with a peace footing of
nearly half a million.   In 1888 it extended
the time of service in the *Landwehr*, increasing the fighting strength of the army
by 700,000 men, and enabling Germany, as
Bismarck said in his great speech of February 8, 1886, to put a million men on each
frontier — the western and the eastern.

The sep-
tennate

During the first years of the new
empire the imperial treasury derived its
income largely from contributions levied
upon the single states. The constitution
assigned to the empire all customs duties,
but under the existing tariff these duties
were quite insufficient to balance the imperial budget. The constitution also gave
the empire wide powers of indirect taxation, and Bismarck resolved to utilize
this source of supply. For such taxation, the most available objects were
spirits and tobacco. An excise upon
spirits would have encountered the opposition of the Conservative landholders,
who are large producers of brandy; and
no measure of financial reform could be
carried without the aid of the Conservatives. Bismarck accordingly turned to
tobacco, and demanded either a monopoly or a heavy taxation of the manufacture. The monopoly was his choice.
He claimed that the tobacco monopoly
would not merely place the empire in
a position of financial independence, but

German
finances

Project of a
tobacco
monopoly

would give it a surplus to be divided among the single states. · The states would thus be enabled to reduce greatly their direct taxes. This project, however, found no favor in the eyes of the German Liberals. The manufacture of tobacco is one of the most prosperous of Germany's industries, and one of the least concentrated. It is carried on in thousands of little factories, and often as a house industry. Accordingly, the National Liberals, who represent especially the middle class, opposed the monopoly. For a time the leaders of this party seemed inclined to support some scheme for taxing the manufacture

Defeat of the project of tobacco; but the opposition of their constituents ultimately forced them into opposition on this point also. Without the support of the National Liberals the proposed taxes could not be carried; for the Conservative and National Liberal parties constituted the majority upon which the government had thus far depended. No feasible way of increasing the imperial receipts was now left except an increase of the customs duties. This involved the abandonment of the policy which the German customs union had pursued from the outset, and to which the empire had thus far remained constant. But Germany was ready for a change. The theory of free trade had been strongly assailed. Numerous industries were clamoring for protection, and to secure a protective tariff it was necessary only to bring a sufficient number of industrial interests into combination. Such a tariff was passed July 12, 1879, by a combination of the land and the iron interests. The duties imposed on breadstuffs and cattle held the Conservatives firm in their allegiance to the government, and the duties on iron won the support of the Ultramontanes, this party being strongly recruited from the mining and manufacturing districts on the Rhine. The National Liberal party was temporarily disrupted. Incidentally, it is almost needless to say, this tariff

A protective tariff, 1879

has been a source of greatly increased
revenue to the empire; and since its
adoption the imperial budget has been
balanced without collecting contributions
from the states. At present the financial
independence of the empire is further
assured by a tax upon spirits, voted
by the strongly governmental Diet of
1887.

Colonial
policy

During the debates upon the tariff of
1879 Bismarck urged that the protection
of German industries would increase not
only the wealth of Germany but its population also, and thus doubly strengthen
the country. Emigration, he argued, was
due to lack of employment, and the
growth of manufactures would increase
the demand for labor and enable more
Germans to live in Germany. But the
chancellor did not expect these results
from the simple imposition of protective
duties. The output of the German
factories could not permanently be increased without an increase of the for-

eign demand. New channels must be
opened to German trade and new mar-
kets conquered for German industry.
Much had been done already by the
private enterprise of German merchants;
much more could be done if their efforts
were seconded by the diplomacy and
supported by the power of the imperial
government. The first step in the development of Bismarck's far-reaching plans
was the sudden seizure in 1884 of a number of points upon the coasts of Africa
and the islands of the Pacific ocean.
The second step was to break down the
exorbitant African claims of Portugal,
and to open the Congo to the commerce
of the world. This was done at the
Berlin conference of 1884–85. A further
measure contemplated by the chancellor
was the creation by imperial subsidies
of German steamship lines which should
give the German manufacturers and merchants rapid and direct communication
with the principal ports of Africa, Australia and Asia. This scheme aroused

The Berlin
conference
1884-85

strong opposition in the German parliament, and Bismarck, after repeatedly renewing his demands, obtained only a portion of the desired subsidies.

General results

If we consider simply the extent to which his direct ends were realized, Bismarck's conduct of the internal politics of the empire seems a mixture of success and failure. But if we consider the degree to which his ultimate purpose was achieved, and in what measure the central power was strengthened and the new national union consolidated, his administration, in its net result, seems altogether successful. When he withdrew from office, he left the empire strong in arms, independent in its finances, and exercising an undisputed sovereignty in legislation and administration.

Foreign relations of the empire 1871-90

The chancellor's conduct of German diplomacy during the early years of the empire is generally recognized as altogether masterly and successful. In this domain, even the most obstinate opponents of his internal administration conceded his supremacy. In its main lines, his foreign policy was extremely simple. Its object was to avert war. Germany had obtained what she desired. She belonged to the satisfied nations. She had nothing to gain by further victories and much to lose by defeat. The chief menace to her peace came, of course, from France. It was impossible for the French people to abandon the hope of reconquering their lost provinces. But they were not likely, as things stood, to declare war without some strengthening alliance. It was therefore the task of the German chancellor to keep France isolated. For this purpose he considered it desirable that France should remain a republic. The establishment of a monarchic government in France would, he believed, make it easier for that country to obtain allies. The attempt of the German ambassador at Paris, Count von Arnim, to carry out an opposite policy and aid the

France

Royalists, was the beginning of the quarrel between the two men which ended in Arnim's ruin.

A more direct means of preserving the peace of Europe was to hold and strengthen Germany's friendships. It was especially important to retain, if possible, the good will of Russia. The friendly attitude assumed by the Russian emperor in 1866 and 1870 had greatly facilitated the unification of Germany. But Russia's friendship was a precarious possession. It rested in part upon the insecure basis of dynastic sympathy, and in part upon a lively expectation of services to be rendered by Germany. It proved difficult for Bismarck to satisfy this expectation. In 1870 Germany helped Russia to set aside the treaty of Paris (1856) and reassert her supremacy in the Black sea; during the Turco-Russian war, in 1877 and 1878, Germany observed a friendly neutrality; and at the Congress of Berlin Bismarck, as "the honest broker," endeavored to mediate fairly between Russia on the one hand and Austria and England on the other, and to save for Russia some of the fruits of her victories. But his support seemed to the Russians insincere. The ill success of the Russian diplomacy was laid at his door; and the relations between the two empires became strained and unfriendly. Bismarck at once opened negotiations with Austria, and in 1879 a treaty of alliance was concluded. This treaty was published in February, 1888. It establishes a defensive alliance for the maintenance of the peace of Europe. It is directed, of course, against the two powers from whom a disturbance of the peace is most to be feared — France and Russia. In 1882, Italy, irritated by the French occupation of Tunis, joined the German-Austrian alliance. Russia apparently deemed it inadvisable to make head against this combination, and externally friendly relations were reëstablished between the courts of Berlin and St. Petersburg. Bismarck, on his part, while holding fast to

German-Austrian alliance, 1879

The triple alliance, 1882

the Austrian alliance, made every effort
to avoid a breach with Russia. From
1884 to 1890 the peace of Europe was
" reinsured " by a secret treaty between
Germany and Russia, in which each
power pledged itself to remain neutral
in case the other should be attacked
by a third power. It appears that the
terms of this treaty were unofficially com-
municated to the governments of Austria
and Italy, but that, at the desire of Russia,
its very existence was kept secret from
France and the other powers. From
1884 to 1890, Germany supported Russia's diplomacy in the Balkan peninsula,
and Austria acted in concert with Germany.

Bismarck
and the old
emperor

Bismarck's relations with William I
had long been satisfactory. The distrust with which the king at first contemplated the rapid resolutions and
apparently rash actions of his minister
had long since disappeared: no distrust
could survive successes so brilliant and

so continuous. If in the long run William realized that it was not he but his
chancellor who was shaping history, his
mind was too just to harbor resentment
and his nature too noble for jealousy.
In course of time, as Marcks asserts and
as we may well believe, William's confidence and gratitude ripened into sincere
affection. After the establishment of
the empire no court intrigues, however
strongly supported, were able seriously
to shake Bismarck's position. The alliance between the government and the
Liberals after 1866 entailed many results
which the emperor did not like; but he
accepted them. The treaty of alliance
with Austria in 1879 seriously distressed
him, because it seemed to destroy all
prospect of cordial relations with Russia;
but he accepted that, too. This was the
last important conflict; during the re-
maining eight years of William's reign
we hear of no more friction between the
emperor and his chancellor.

The death of William I and the brief

G

reign of Frederick III wrought no change in the position or power of the chancellor. The humane and idealistic Frederick had little sympathy with Bismarck's rough and often cynical realism, but he showed no disposition to discharge a minister who had rendered such services to the dynasty and the nation. Bismarck had. equally little sympathy with such a character as Frederick's; but he stood ready to serve the son as loyally as he had served the father. Frederick's posthumous diary exhibits in the strongest light this antagonism of temperaments, and his own incapacity to understand Bismarck; but it also shows us how completely the stronger will, when it chose to make the effort, dominated the weaker. Had Frederick ascended the throne in full health of body and vigor of mind, the struggle for power which showed itself in his reign might have assumed larger proportions and a more acute character; but it would still have been a struggle, not between the king and his minister, but between the minister and other wills striving to impose themselves upon the king.

Whatever peril of a breach existed was thought to be removed when William II became emperor. The new ruler was but twenty-nine years old; he had grown up during the triumphs of Bismarck's diplomacy; it was understood that he shared, or reflected, Bismarck's views. But it soon became clear that the young emperor had ideas and a will of his own, and was not inclined to be guided by an all-powerful premier. To an energetic disposition he added the conviction of a personal responsibility to be discharged by personal attention to all governmental affairs. The question soon arose whether Bismarck, as president of the Prussian ministry, was to continue to exercise the powers of a premier as he understood them, or whether the monarch, to use Bismarck's expression, was "himself to act as minister-president." A Prussian ordinance of nearly forty

William II
1888

Ministerial
vs. imperial
responsibility

years' standing required that all communication between the king and his
ministers should pass through the president of the ministry. During the long
reign of William I this ordinance had
been so fully observed, in the letter and
in the spirit, that the minister-president
alone was directly responsible to the
king; the other ministers were practically responsible to the premier. In the
winter of 1889–90 Bismarck became
aware that certain members of the Prussian ministry were working against him,
and he promptly demanded that the ordinance of 1852 be enforced. This demand the emperor met with a proposal
that the ordinance in question should be
revoked. To this proposal Bismarck
refused his ministerial consent. The
emperor apparently acquiesced in this
decision; but he demanded shortly after-
wards that Bismarck should keep him
informed of all negotiations with members of parliament. This Bismarck
refused to promise; and after an angry

discussion on March 17, 1890, the emperor demanded Bismarck's resignation. The immediate cause of this quarrel was an interview between Bismarck and Windthorst, in which, according to Bismarck's friends, Windthorst offered the chancellor the support of the Centre against the emperor, — an offer which the chancellor declined to consider, — while, according to the story that reached the emperor's ears, it was Bismarck who was seeking such an alliance against his imperial master. Bismarck at first refused to resign and demanded an open dismissal; but in response to a second demand he tendered his resignation, which was immediately accepted. A few days later the ex-chancellor left Berlin amid great demonstrations of popular affection and regret. In 1866 Bismarck was upheld by the king alone against almost universal hatred and distrust. He had now lost the support of the crown, but he had won the confidence and the love of the German people.

Windthorst interview

Bismarck's enforced resignation March 20 1890

The quarrel
with the
emperor
The quarrel between the ex-chancellor
and the emperor soon became open and
bitter. In inspired editorials and personal interviews Bismarck subjected the
policy pursued by his successor, General
Caprivi, to detailed and often scathing
criticism. It was notorious, however, that
William had now become his own premier
and that the measures fathered by Caprivi
were really William's; and the emperor re-
torted with circular notes to the foreign
powers, explaining that no weight was
to be attached to Bismarck's utterances.
There appeared also semi-official threats
of prosecution for libel or for treason,
which were wisely left unrealized. All
that the emperor could do, in fact, was
to place Bismarck under a social ban, as
far as court functions and public cere-
monies were concerned, to request foreign courts to withhold from him and
his family all social recognition, and to
withdraw from Bismarck's friends and
admirers all governmental favors and
privileges.

To the great relief of the German peo- ple, this unseemly contest was ended by a public and formal reconciliation. A severe illness by which the prince was attacked in the summer of 1893 facilitated overtures on the part of the emperor. They were cordially received; and in January, 1894, amid demonstrations of lively popular satisfaction, the dismissed servant and his imperial master exchanged visits at Berlin and Friedrichsruh, with much of the state and ceremony which surrounds the intercourse of potentates of equal rank. In the following year the emperor figured prominently in the celebration of Bis- marck's eightieth birthday. An imperial visit to Friedrichsruh opened a series of demonstrations which were protracted for a fortnight, and which were compressed within that period only by the orders of Bismarck's physicians. Representative delegations came from all parts of the empire; addresses and gifts poured in, not only from Germany and the German colonies, but from every considerable body of German-speaking residents in foreign lands. The only discordant note in this national festival was the refusal of the Imperial Diet, controlled by Bismarck's old antagonists, Ultramontanes, Particularists, Radicals and Social Democrats, to pass a formal vote of congratulation; but this refusal evoked so general an outburst of popular indignation that the incident helped to emphasize the reverence and affection of the German people for their great statesman.

The closing years of Bismarck's life were passed in domestic retirement, although to the very end he maintained a close watch upon the course of contemporary politics and occasionally expressed his views through the columns
Death of the *Hamburger Nachrichten.* He died July 30, 1898, leaving instructions that he be interred without pomp upon his estate at Friedrichsruh, and that upon his tomb be inscribed: " A faithful German servant of Emperor William I."

Before his retirement from power, Bismarck had received, both from the king
whom he made emperor and from the
people whom he made into a nation,
many substantial tokens of appreciation
and gratitude. After the conclusion of
the Gastein convention William I conferred upon him the title of count, and
when the German empire was established
that of prince. The king also gave him
the estate of Friedrichsruh in Lauenburg.
In 1866, when the government proposed
to the Prussian Diet the bestowal of
dotations upon Moltke, Roon and other
generals, the Diet, of its own motion,
placed Bismarck's name at the head of
the list, and voted him the largest sum —
400,000 thalers ($288,000). In 1871, in
connection with a similar series of dotations, the Imperial Diet voted him 750,000
thalers ($540,000). In 1885, when the
prince completed his seventieth year, the
sum of 2,379,143.94 marks (nearly $571,-
000) was raised by popular subscription.
The committee which received the sub-

scription expended 1,150,000 marks in the redemption of a part of the estate of Schönhausen, sold by the prince's father. The letter of presentation declared it a fitting thing that Germany, to which the prince had restored so much of its lost territory, should restore to the prince the lands held by his ancestors. The remainder of the fund was converted, at the prince's desire, into a perpetual foundation for the support of candidates for appointment in the higher institutions of learning and for the relief of the widows of teachers in such institutions. In 1890, in accepting Bismarck's resignation, William II conferred upon him the title of duke of Lauenburg and advanced him to high military rank. The emperor also offered him, as a pension, the continuance of his official salary; but this offer was rejected.

Personal characteristics   Bismarck was a man of great stature — six feet and two inches, English measure —and of athletic frame. In his youth and early manhood he was an excellent fencer, a powerful swimmer and a tireless rider; and at the age of fifty-five he bore the exposure and fatigue of the winter campaign in France not merely without injury but with positive benefit to his health. In later years his increasing weight unfitted him for physical exertion; but his capacity for protracted mental labor, always phenomenal, was unimpaired at the close of his public career.

He possessed strong social instincts and great social talents. The perception of the characteristic in men and in things, the faculty of sketching in words, the frequent wit and the constant caustic humor which made him one of the best of letter-writers, made him also one of the best of talkers. This talent he turned to good account, not in European diplomacy only but in German politics as well. Many questions that could not be settled by debates in parliament were adjusted over the beer and in the smoke of his famous parliamentary breakfasts in the Wilhelmstrasse.

Speeches He was not commonly regarded by the Germans as a good parliamentary speaker. In England he would have been regarded as one of the best. The German taste in public speaking inclines to the oratorical; Bismarck's manner was usually conversational. The substance and the arrangement of his speeches were excellent. They were always adapted rather to convince his hearers than to excite their admiration. They contained, nevertheless, more quotable sayings and have enriched the speech of Germany with more quotations, not, perhaps, than the writings of her great poets but certainly than the spoken words of any German since Luther.

Writings His writings have not only the excellence often observed in men of action — the simplicity, directness and vigor of a Wellington or a Grant — they have in high degree a distinctively literary quality and charm. The vague word is avoided, and the precise, unique word is found; the current phrase, that has lost its edges by wear, is replaced by a phrase fresh-

minted and clean-cut; there is the unexpected turn that is wit without the
obvious intention, and the literary suggestion that is not quotation; there is
everywhere the perception not only of
the intellectual but also of the sensuous
value of words — in sum, there is style.
When Bismarck's letters were first published, the poet and novelist Heyse is said
to have thanked God that that man had
gone into politics, "because he would
have spoiled our trade."

The qualities that distinguished Bis- Qualities as a
marck as a statesman were rapid and statesman
accurate perception of the central and
decisive points in the most complicated
situation; tenacity of purpose in following
his chief end, combined with readiness to
vary, with every change of circumstances,
the mode of its pursuit; and a rare degree
of moderation at the moment of fullest
triumph. Of this last trait he gave strik-
ing evidence in the terms accorded to
Austria and to the Prussian parliamentary
opposition after the victories of 1866.

Political methods In the earlier stages especially of his public career, Bismarck showed himself a master of diplomatic strategy, but where finesse seemed needless he often employed methods that savored of brutality. It should, however, be remembered that the belated political development of Germany forced upon him, in an age that is humane to the verge of sentimentalism, the rough work which William the Conqueror did for England in the eleventh century and Richelieu for France in the seventeenth. One great merit of his diplomacy was its general truthfulness; nor is this merit lessened by the fact that, because of the persistence of an opposite tradition, Bismarck's frankness was often more deceptive than another man's lies.

Family Bismarck was married in 1847 to Johanna von Puttkammer, to whose constant sympathy, unwavering confidence and watchful care the prince declared himself largely indebted for his successes. Of this union three children were born

— the Countess Marie, born in 1848, and married to Count Cuno Rantzau; Count Herbert, born in 1849, and married in 1892 to Marguerite, Countess Hoyos; and Count William, born in 1852, and married in 1885 to Sibylla von Arnim, whose mother was a Bismarck. Of each of these unions children have been born. Count Herbert, now the second Prince Bismarck, was a member of the Prussian cabinet when his father was dismissed, and withdrew with him from the service of the crown. He has since sat as a Conservative in the Imperial Diet. Count William is president of the district of Hanover in the province of the same name.

The literature dealing directly or chiefly with the life and achievements of Prince Bismarck is already very extensive. His speeches have been published in several German editions — the best is Kohl's, in twelve volumes — and in a French edition of fifteen volumes. Many of his diplomatic and other state papers have been

Bismarck literature

published by Poschinger — *Preussen im Bundestage*, four volumes; *Dokumente zur Geschichte der Wirthschaftspolitik*, five volumes — and by Hahn and Wippermann in *Fürst Bismarck*, five volumes. Four volumes of Bismarck's political letters and four small volumes of his private letters have also been printed. It is announced that the prince left memoirs to be published at the discretion of his successor. In Busch — *Bismarck und seine Leute, Neue Tagebuchblätter, Unser Reichs-Kanzler, Bismarck und sein Werk* — the prince found a Boswell who kept a diary and who reports much of the great man's small-talk. Bismarck's Frankfort despatches and his letters have been translated into French; some of his letters have also appeared in English. Busch's material has recently been collected and published in English in two large volumes: *Bismarck: Some Secret Pages of his History* (1898).

The best account of Bismarck's public career down to 1870 is that given by

Sybel in his *Begründung des deutschen Reichs*, seven volumes, of which there is an English translation. Sybel's history is based, except as regards the years 1867–70, upon the Prussian archives; and until these and other European archives are thrown open to students, it will remain the most authoritative source of information. The fullest study of Bismarck's policy after 1870 is given by Blum in his *Deutsches Reich zur Zeit Bismarcks* — a book largely inspired by the prince himself. Blum has also published an elaborate history in six volumes, covering Bismarck's entire career: *Bismarck und seine Zeit*. Numerous other biographies of Bismarck have been written by his countrymen; those by Hesekiel, Müller and Jahnke seem to be the most popular. The best French book is that by Edouard Simon; the fullest English life is Charles Lowe's *Prince Bismarck*, two volumes, 1886. Mr. Lowe has since published a more condensed biography in one volume.

H

Those who are curious to follow the changing appreciations of Bismarck as revealed in caricatures will find collected in one volume — *Bismarck-Album des Kladderadatsch* — all the Bismarck pictures published by the leading humorous paper of Berlin, from the first appearance of the Prussian deputy in 1847 to the dismissal of the German chancellor in 1890; and in Grand-Carteret, *Bismarck en Caricatures* (Paris, 1890), they will find reproductions of one hundred and forty cartoons from comic papers in all parts of the world.

In his little *Bismarck-Gedenkbuch* (1888) Kohl gives a fairly full Bismarck bibliography, and also a list of original paintings, sketches and photographs of the prince. A relatively complete bibliography by Schultze and Koller — *Bismarck-Literatur*, Leipsic, 1895 — contains about six hundred titles. Lemcke and Buechner of New York publish a useful list of selected books and pamphlets.

Since 1893 a *Bismarck-Jahrbuch* has

appeared, edited by Kohl and devoted exclusively to the study of Bismarck's life and achievements.

Modern German and European histories; German political pamphlets from 1862 to the present time; memoirs and biographies of the German statesmen and generals who were associated with Bismarck's work and of the foreigners who were his allies or his enemies — all these necessarily deal to a greater or less extent with Bismarck's career and constitute a sort of secondary Bismarck literature. Among the works of the last-mentioned class — memoirs and biographies — one deserves special mention, not only because its author has much to say about Bismarck, but also because of the fairness and insight that he displays. This book, which has already been cited in the foregoing sketch, is Erich Marcks's *Kaiser Wilhelm I.*

SCIENCE OF STATISTICS, PART I

STATISTICS AND SOCIOLOGY

By RICHMOND MAYO-SMITH, Ph.D.,

Professor of Political Economy and Social Science in Columbia College

8vo. Cloth. pp. xvi. + 399. $3.00, net

Sociology is the science which treats of social organization. It has for object of research the laws which seem to underlie the relations of men in society. It studies social phenomena. But the sociologist meets two great difficulties ; one is the enormous number and complexity of these social phenomena, and the second is the lack of any precise means of measuring or gauging social forces. History and observation give us general knowledge of these phenomena. In some directions one can reach quantitative measurements in addition to mere qualitative description. This is done by means of statistics. The science of Statistics is therefore one of the most important instruments of investigation in Sociology.

The object of this book is to show how Statistics should be used by the sociologist and to give some of the results thus far attained. In each chapter special emphasis is laid on the right use of the method, and the ordinary fallacies and misuse of statistics are carefully pointed out. The object is to furnish the student of sociology and the general reader with the most interesting facts and at the same time to make him competent to judge of the value of the evidence.

The material gathered in this volume is all included under Population Statistics. It deals with the classification of population according to sex, age, and conjugal condition, with births, marriages, deaths, sickness, and mortality ; the social condition of the community is considered under the statistics of families, dwellings, education, religious confession, infirmities, suicide, and crime ; ethnographic problems are dealt with under race and nationality, migration, population and land (physical environment), and population and civilization (social environment). The causes affecting each phenomenon, *e.g.* scarcity of food, and crime, are carefully considered in each case.

The author has utilized the material furnished by the recent American and European censuses of 1890 and 1891 which has just become accessible. This material will not be superseded for ten years at least. For current statistics such as births, marriages, and deaths he has used the averages for the decade 1880–90 as being typical rather than the figures for a single year. While the book is not a manual of statistics in the ordinary sense, it contains all the important facts about population critically arranged and analyzed. The reader is not sent adrift among a lot of tables, but the relation of the facts to each other is carefully observed. At the same time a topical index makes the book useful as a dictionary of population statistics.

The present volume is issued as Part I. of a systematic Science of Statistics, and is intended to cover what is ordinarily termed Population Statistics. The author has in preparation Part II., Statistics and Economics, which will cover the statistics of commerce, trade, finance, and economic social life generally.

CONTENTS.

THE MACMILLAN COMPANY

66 FIFTH AVENUE, NEW YORK

FROM THE PRESS.

" Professor Mayo-Smith's long-expected work on statistics is sure to take front rank in the literature of the subject in the English language. It is not a book of statistical references, but is rather a work devoted to the interpretation of statistical data. . . . The success which greeted Professor Mayo-Smith's earlier sketch, ' Statistics and Economics,' will doubtless be accorded in still greater measure to his more ambitious effort. The situation of our statistical literature is such that even a poor performance in this field would be of importance. A work which has the scholarly character of the present volume can count upon an assured success." — *Annals of the American Academy of Political and Social Science.*

" It embodies the conclusions of a pioneer in the field, who has been lecturing on statistics for a dozen years at Columbia College, and who, by his teaching and influence, has contributed to arouse an enlightened interest in the subject. This work will extend and deepen that interest among students of affairs; and by providing a text-book, which might be used for a class either with or without supplementary lectures, it should make the introduction of the subject into the curricula of other institutions possible. This volume contains the only full statement in the English language of the general principles and conclusions of statistics, and it is a matter of congratulation that an American scholar should be the first to offer such a work to the public."— *The Educational Review.*

"An exceedingly useful work. . . . From a vast range of reliable sources Professor Mayo-Smith, an expert in statistical methods, has brought together a mass of ordered materials which bear on social problems ; and students of sociology are deeply his debtors. Many vague notions and insecure theories will be tested by the yard-stick of this book, and no serious workers can afford to ignore it. . . . It is a distinct merit of the work that the data compiled are arranged in a way to excite interest and lead to results."— *The Dial.*

" No more important work bearing on the subject of social science has been issued recently. In 1890 and 1891 full and complete censuses were taken in the United States, England, Scotland, Ireland, Germany, France, Austria, and India, and Professor Mayo-Smith has availed himself of the results of these to present in intelligible and scientific form such of the statistics as bear directly upon the most important and vital sociological and economical questions of the day, which are pressing themselves home not only upon students, sociologists, and publicists, but upon intelligent men generally. . . . In brief, the book may be accepted as an authority, and its value, filling a place too long vacant in the literature of sociological science, is not easily exaggerated." — *Boston Daily Advertiser.*

" Far from being an arid text-book, these statistical facts are so systematically arranged and presented, with such ingenious and instructive comment, as to furnish in small compass a vast magazine of curious facts with no little interesting reading, at least to any one taking the slightest interest in sociology. The indexing cannot be too highly commended, rendering, as it does, a wide range of statistics instantly available."— *The Milwaukee Sentinel.*

" The work is a novelty in American literature, nothing of the kind ever having been before issued. It is also a model of method and ought to be as safe a guide as the mariner's compass has been to the navigator in the past. . . . While the author has published a text-book for the student and a guide for the statistician, he has also issued a very interesting work for common perusal." — *The Detroit Tribune.*

THE MACMILLAN COMPANY

66 FIFTH AVENUE, NEW YORK

MUNICIPAL HOME RULE.

A Study in Administration.

BY

FRANK J. GOODNOW, LL.D.,

Professor of Administrative Law, Columbia University in the City of New York.

Cloth. 16mo. $1.50, net.

COMMENTS.

"Indeed, we doubt if any author has achieved such eminent success in the solution of the difficult problems of city government as the author of the present work." — *Times-Union*, Albany, N.Y.

"A scholarly, thoughtful, and independent criticism of municipal experiences and the plans now urged to better municipal conditions. . . . The volume is an exceptionally valuable one to close students of municipal affairs." — *Outlook*.

"Every one interested in municipal reform, and the possibility of securing honest and effective government for American cities, ought by all means to give studious attention to Professor Goodnow's philosophical presentation of the subject." — *Boston Beacon*.

"It is one of the finest studies in administration that has ever been offered to political students." — *Inter-Ocean*.

THE MACMILLAN COMPANY,

66 FIFTH AVENUE, NEW YORK.

MUNICIPAL PROBLEMS.

BY

FRANK J. GOODNOW, LL.D.,

*Professor of Administrative Law, Columbia University
in the City of New York.*

Cloth. 16mo. $1.50, net.

COMMENTS.

"We question if any other book before has achieved quite the important service to what may be termed theoretic municipalism. . . . One that all those interested in municipal matters should read. . . . Moderate in tone, sound in argument, and impartial in its conclusions, it is a work that deserves to carry weight." — *London Liberal.*

"Here is without doubt one of the most trenchant and scholarly contributions to political science of recent writing, remarkable for analytical power and lucidity of statement." — *Chicago Evening Post.*

THE MACMILLAN COMPANY,
66 FIFTH AVENUE, NEW YORK.

PUBLICATIONS OF THE COLUMBIA UNIVERSITY PRESS

CLASSICAL STUDIES

IN HONOUR OF

HENRY DRISLER

WITH PORTRAIT AND ILLUSTRATIONS

8vo. Cloth. pp. viii + 310. $4.00, net

CONTENTS

On the meaning of *nauta* and *viator* in Horace, Sat. I. 5, 11-23. By SIDNEY
G. ASHMORE. — Anaximander on the Prolongation of Infancy in Man. By
NICHOLAS MURRAY BUTLER. — Of Two Passages in Euripides' Medea. By
MORTIMER LAMSON EARLE. — The Preliminary Military Service of the
Equestrian Cursus Honorum. By JAMES C. EGBERT, Jr. — References to
Zoroaster in Syriac and Arabic Literature. By RICHARD J. H. GOTTHEIL. —
Literary Frauds among the Greeks. By ALFRED GUDEMAN. — Henotheism in
the Rig-Veda. By EDWARD WASHBURN HOPKINS. — On Plato and the Attic
Comedy. By GEORGE B. HUSSEY. — Herodotus VII. 61, or Ancient Persian
Armour. By A. V. WILLIAMS JACKSON. — Archaism in Aulus Gellius. By
CHARLES KNAPP. — On Certain Parallelisms between the Ancient and the
Modern Drama. BY BRANDER MATTHEWS. — Ovid's Use of Colour and
Colour-Terms. By NELSON GLENN McCREA. — A Bronze of Polyclitan
Affinities in the Metropolitan Museum. By A. C. MERRIAM. — Geryon
in Cyprus. By A. C. MERRIAM. — Hercules, Hydra, and the Crab. By
A. C. MERRIAM. — Onomatopoetic Words in Latin. By H. T. PECK. — Notes
on the Vedic Deity Pūṣan. By E. D. PERRY. — The So-Called Medusa
Ludovisi. By JULIUS SACHS. — Aristotle and the Arabs. By WILLIAM M.
SLOANE. — Iphigenia in Greek and French Tragedy. By BENJAMIN DURYEA
WOODWARD. — Gargettus, an Attic Deme. By C. H. YOUNG.

THE MACMILLAN COMPANY

66 FIFTH AVENUE, NEW YORK

FROM THE PRESS

"Many glimpses of fields almost untrodden in Greek and Latin literature are given in this volume." — *The New York Tribune.*

"A recent publication which will appeal to every American scholar. . . . The papers are kept strictly within the lines of scholarship and criticism in which Dr. Drisler himself has been engaged. On the part of the contributors they are an offering of what is choicest and best in their own profession, a rich and delightful mosaic of American scholarship, which will bear study part by part, and which, in the combined setting of the parts, is an incomparable tribute to the incomparable Nestor of our American Greek schools." — *The Independent.*

"The circumstances of the issue of this handsome volume give it an emotional interest, which makes it a volume separate and distinct among the collected records of the investigations of scholars. It is a gathering of twenty-one studies of classical problems, printed as a tribute to one of the best-known classical students of the present day, at the conclusion of fifty years of his service in a single institution. . . . These circumstances give this volume an interest to all persons concerned with scholarship and university influences. The studies themselves, for the most part, appeal in the first instance to specialists, but many of them have a much wider interest. . . . The book is a credit to American scholarship, as well as a fit tribute to the honored name of Professor Drisler." — *The Outlook.*

"Entirely apart from the special interest which its contents possess for the student of the classics, the publication of this handsomely printed volume has some features that are of general significance. It gives evidence, for one thing, of the Germanization of our classical scholars, not only in their methods of research and the other weightier matters of the law, but also in the minor points of academic custom and tradition. In Germany it has long been the practice for the friends and former pupils of a distinguished scholar to celebrate some epoch of his career by the publication, in his honor, of a collection of scientific monographs relating to the special subjects in which his life-work has been spent and his reputation won. . . . So far as the writer knows, the work that has just appeared from the new Columbia University Press — the first to be issued by that organization — is the only one of the kind yet published in honor of an English-speaking scholar. . . . This collection of monographs is particularly instructive as practically illustrating the economic principle of the division of labor applied to scholarly pursuits. The stock charge that has been brought against the intense and minute specialization of the present day, is that specialists in their devotion, each to his own limited field of research, lose their sense of perspective, despise the equally important labors of their fellow-specialists, and come to feel that the part is greater than the whole. Such a volume as the present affords a practical and ample refutation of that view. Here we see investigators in many different fields of study, not only using in their own work the garnered results of other specialists, but ably and effectively throwing upon the problems of other workers the special knowledge that their own research has enabled them to give. . . . The appearance of the volume is unusually attractive and reflects credit upon the Columbia University Press, whose work of publication is thus so appropriately and so auspiciously begun." — *The Educational Review.*

THE MACMILLAN COMPANY
66 FIFTH AVENUE, NEW YORK